"CHRIST SHALL PROFIT YOU NOTHING!"

THE CHURCH OF GOD

Moreno Dal Bello

"CHRIST SHALL PROFIT YOU NOTHING!"

A false gospel is not to be judged so when its errors reach a certain point, but in the fact that it contains any error at all! Doctrinal error is indicative of a false gospel. All false gospels *take away from* or *add to* what God says and all believers in such pockmarked messages scarred with error are lost. One of the clearest examples of how little it takes to besmirch God's Gospel and change it into a lie is shown by Paul in his letter to the Galatians. **"Behold, I Paul say unto you, that if ye be circumcised, CHRIST SHALL PROFIT YOU NOTHING"** (Gal. 5:2). Paul made it clear to his hearers then, and it should be just as clear to his hearers now, that **if a person turns to and relies upon anything that they have done in order to get saved and/or remain saved then Christ shall profit them nothing.** It will be folly for them to call on the Lord Jesus, whose obedience alone saves, when they believe *their own* obedience to be an essential ingredient in their salvation. Any gospel that contains such doctrine is not from God and therefore cannot save. Paul does not say that Christ will forgive their error because they meant well or for their sincerity of heart, or because they believed in more true doctrines than false, but Paul makes it perfectly clear that Christ shall not profit them in the slightest. He cannot be called on as Savior by these people for they do not fully trust in Him. They can shout His name all they like; they can claim to be believers in grace and even know 'Amazing Grace' off by heart, but those who believe that any part of salvation is conditioned on anything a man must do, **even those who claim that whatever it is they must do is only possible because of God's bestowing the grace which enables them to do it,** are abiders in a false gospel, a gospel which is not about grace but may be rightly termed a **gospel of DIS-GRACE!!**

Earlier in his letter, the apostle Paul left his readers with no doubt in their minds, and with nothing else to conclude, as to the state of those who would bring a gospel which differed **in any way, to any degree,** with what he had told them: *"But though we, or an angel from heaven, preach any other gospel unto you than that which we have preached unto you, let him be accursed. As we said before, so say I now again, If any man preach any other gospel unto you than that ye have received, let him be accursed"* (Gal. 1:8,9). They were accursed people, and their gospels nothing but rank imitations, who believed in a gospel which strayed one hair's breadth from the Gospel Paul had received from God. Paul's succinct statements regarding what the Gospel was and what it was not shows the simple reasoning of the inspired apostle, that if what a person presented to the Galatians was not what he had told them, if they did not agree with Paul's Gospel or claimed to be teaching it *yet added to it or took away from it one jot or tittle,* it would no longer be what God had told Paul and would therefore qualify as *another* gospel.

The strongest evidence for this, that even the smallest or slightest deviation from the truth, from what God has said in His Gospel, from the record that HE bears of HIS Son (1 Jn. 5:10), qualifies a person's gospel as something *other than* God's Gospel, is found further on in Paul's letter in the following key verse: **"A little leaven leaveneth the whole lump"** (Gal. 5:9). Leaven, as seen in Matthew 16, is symbolical of teaching. *"By leaven the Hebrews metaphorically understood whatever had the power of corrupting, whether doctrine, or example or anything else....Leaven is used in making bread. Its use is to pass through the flour, and cause it to ferment or to swell, and become light. It passes secretly, silently, but certainly."* Paul warned that a **little** leaven will leaven the **whole** lump. The word *little* here comes from the Greek word *mikros* from which we get our word *micro*, meaning **very small.** This is proof positive that even the slightest error when it comes to the Gospel is enough to brand that message a false gospel. How could it not be so? For instance, if one has 4 toy blocks, the only way it can be said that they are the same is if they are *exactly* the same. If there are any differences between them, even the slightest scratch, then the most that can be said is that they are *similar* but it can never be said that they are the *same*. **If there is anything different about a gospel, anything in it which differs from that great Gospel of God, it is a gospel that cannot save and God will not tolerate anyone who believes in anything that differs from His Gospel!! After all, isn't salvation about believing what GOD has said and repenting of what man's doctrines teach, of everything that contradicts what God has said?** God does not stray from His truth, He does not change, nor has His message of how He saves changed. His message does not contain error of any size and so any message that does contain even the most minute error cannot be God's Message, God's Gospel. **And those who believe in such messages cannot be said to be God's people for how can it be said that they have been given justifying faith if they believe a false gospel, which is what justifying faith is sent to free God's people from? You are never a Christian before the faith that comes from God, which believes only His Gospel and rejects all others, is given to you.** How can faith in a false gospel be said to justify a man when it obviously could not have been given by God for it does not believe all that God has said?

But why is this so and how can we recognize a false gospel? Well, the reason even the slightest error when it comes to what the Gospel is, that is God's plan for the salvation of His people, is that God's Gospel is the only Gospel which bases salvation completely on grace, ie. **upon nothing we do but solely on what He has done.** Now one can begin to understand how the slightest variation, the slightest modification, of God's Gospel can be easily seen and recognized and the significance of what it means to God's **grace-based** plan. It may be asked, *'But what is it which even in its smallest form can so distort the Gospel of God as to render it a perverted gospel of which He is not the Author and which is unable to save anyone? What is it that Paul is talking about when he speaks of a little leaven leavening the whole lump?'* The answer is a very simple one. God's Gospel is a grace Gospel, it is a Gospel which conditions **all** of salvation—from beginning to final glory—upon His grace. **Grace is what God has done, not what we do.** Salvation is by grace through faith so that none may boast that they have done anything to get or remain saved. **Grace is a gift, Faith is a gift and Salvation is a gift. *"Where is boasting then? It is excluded. By what law? Of works? NAY: but by the law of FAITH"*** (Rom. 3:27). **This exclusion of all boasting on the part of man is concrete evidence that NO PART of salvation could possibly be conditioned on man!** ONLY THE GOSPEL OF **TOTAL GRACE** EXCLUDES THE POSSIBILITY OF ANY MAN BOASTING IN SOMETHING HE HAS DONE—EVEN IF, LIKE THE PHARISEE (Lk. 18:11-14), HE ATTRIBUTES HIS OBEDIENCE TO GOD. The grace of God is not about Him enabling us to do anything, but about Him doing EVERYTHING to save His people from their sins. Therefore salvation is not about us, it is not about what **we** must do, but what **God** has done to secure the salvation of His people. And so, the Savior, God's Holy Servant sent to save those people God had elected before the foundation of the world, was sent to save those people not based on anything they did or that He would enable them to do for themselves, **but by what He would do for them.** Thus all boasting is excluded because salvation comes by grace through faith in the Savior's Works. We conclude from this that that which strays from the first principal of grace—**God doing for those who cannot do for themselves**—is that leaven which the apostle talks about which corrupts the whole message of grace. **A thing cannot be corrupted by itself, therefore grace cannot corrupt grace. It is that which is foreign to a thing which corrupts it and in the case of the grace of God, only the doctrine of the *works* of man can corrupt it. Grace and works are arch enemies, they cannot mix for the one cancels out the other. They are diametrically and eternally opposed. One exalts God alone and the other exalts only man. Therefore, any gospel which stipulates that any part of salvation is conditioned upon what a man does or what he must refrain from doing, leaves room for a man to boast. It is not a gospel of grace but a gospel of works. IF YOU BELIEVE THAT SALVATION DEPENDS IN ANY WAY TO ANY DEGREE UPON YOU, THEN THE GOSPEL YOU BELIEVE IN, HOWEVER MUCH 'GRACE' IT APPEARS TO CONTAIN, IS A GOSPEL OF WORKS.** Election is according to nothing but grace *"And if by grace, then is it no more of works: otherwise grace is no more grace. But if it be of works, then is it no more grace..."* (Rom. 11:6). You cannot have a grace and works Gospel. It is either one or the other. **If it is conditioned on Christ and what He has done then it is the Gospel of grace, but if any part of it is in any way conditioned on what you do then it is a gospel of works and those who believe in such gospels are still in their sins.** A gospel that declares any part of salvation to be dependant upon what a man must do is not the Gospel of grace which comes from God but is a gospel of works invented and believed by lost men. Grace and works are like oil and water in that they simply cannot mix. The above Scripture makes clear that if salvation relies upon a man's works then it cannot be a salvation by grace and if salvation is of grace then you may put your mind at rest in the knowledge that no part of one's salvation is, or was ever, based upon what you do. Salvation is not by grace *and* works, but is by grace alone. **The satanic form of grace is that which the Pharisee in Luke 18, and all like him, had fallen for: God enabling the sinner to obey enough to contribute to his/her salvation.** This form of grace does not exalt God but man, for it does not come from God. **It is not all about God but what God can do for you.**

What Paul was saying in the context of Galatians 5 was that even if the Galatians claimed to believe the Gospel of God's grace yet added, for instance, something as seemingly benign as the doctrine which teaches circumcision as a necessary rite that had to be performed in order for a man to be or remain saved, the Gospel of grace would be perverted, their hearts would belong to *another* gospel, and Christ would profit them nothing: **"Behold, I Paul say unto you, that if ye be circumcised, Christ shall profit you NOTHING"** (Gal. 5:2). NOT A LITTLE, mind you, BUT NOTHING! This shows clearly that even if a person claimed to believe the Gospel, all the right doctrines, yet added anything to it, the true Christ of the true Gospel would be of no advantage to them. Any error added to truth makes it an untruth, so, too, any work added to grace makes it 'un-grace', or non-grace, not something undeserved but something God would be obligated to provide.

An appeal by such people to Christ and what He did on the cross will fall on deaf ears for they have turned their heads and hearts to something outside of, and in addition to, what Christ has done, thereby revealing a lack of confidence in the efficaciousness of Christ and what He has done to save, or an ignorance of Him as complete Savior and the sufficiency of His imputed Righteousness to save. Scripture says that the Righteousness that saves is obtainable only by faith in that Righteousness, in what Christ has done and not by what we do. Those who are ignorant of this Righteousness have no option and therefore feel compelled to go about, as the Jews did in Romans

10, to establish their *own* righteousness, which is what a person does when they consider any part of salvation to be conditioned on what they do. They **"...have not submitted themselves unto the Righteousness of God"** (Rom. 10:3) which comes by grace through faith and not works, lest any man should boast (see Eph. 2:8,9). This absence of trust in, or ignorance of, the Savior's Work is so pronounced, it is such a corruptive influence, that it tries to tempt Paul's hearers to return to the mind-set that is common to every man by nature, which instructs them to look to what *they* do to obtain or to ensure the completeness of their salvation. **One cannot dare to claim to be saved by grace if one believes one has contributed by some act of personal obedience to their 'salvation'.** This is not some minor issue that needs correcting in those that are saved, but is a life and death issue. **It is something that needs to be purged from the lost man, not corrected in the saved man, for no saved man could possibly believe such a deadly error. As we shall see later, it is not by a man's deeds of the law that he is saved, but by Christ's deeds performed on behalf of the man.**

     A dependence upon anything outside of Christ, including any degree of self-reliance to secure or ensure one's salvation, *"...AMOUNTS TO A REJECTION OF THE SAVIOR, AND OF THE DOCTRINE OF JUSTIFICATION BY HIM."* If you add anything to Christ then you erase Christ from the equation and He will profit you nothing. Anything you add to Christ always blocks out Christ, it obscures a right view of the true Christ leaving only oneself in the picture. **Christ profits them nothing who believe in anything apart from, less than, or in addition to, what He has done as that which is necessary to save.** This, however, does not mean that all those who believe in such lies reject all of Christianity, that they abhor all the doctrine of Christ. **False gospels are made up of many truths.** There is almost no end to the subtleties of Satan and his 'greatest' work of perversion, that thing which has deceived more people than anything Evolution, Atheism, Agnosticism or any overtly anti-Christian philosophy or religion could conjure up—**the lie— which stems from Satan's original lie to Eve in the Garden that she would not surely die** (spiritually as well as physically), **that man must do, in turn giving birth to the lie that he CAN do, something which will result in his salvation.** What Paul is talking about is the conditioning of any part of salvation, thus believing there is a need for a man to add his obedience, on something he has to do, to make even 'more perfect' what Christ has done to secure the salvation of His people. Those who truly believe in grace are content with what Christ has done and those who believe they must do something too are malcontents—discontent and unsatisfied with the Savior God has provided. **If you believe you must do something to secure or maintain a state of justification before God, then you are a subscriber to, and**

promoter of, the lie that dares say that Who Christ is and what He has done is not enough to save anyone. Significantly, if you are of the opinion that anyone who believes in a gospel that says man must choose God, thereby conditioning salvation ultimately upon a free will decision on the part of man, you are as lost as anyone can be for you deny Christ by insisting that a person can believe a works-based gospel whose savior shares the glory for salvation with man, and be saved regardless. **There are more ways to deny Christ than the obvious. However subtle they may be they are nonetheless very real and very deadly!**

Paul was saying to the Galatians in chapter 5 that they could claim Christ all they wanted to, call out to Him, 'defend' His name, do all sorts of wonderful works in His name and even cast out devils, but if they added circumcision, something they did, as essential to salvation, to God's Gospel of grace, then it was *another* gospel. It was not the Gospel of grace but a gospel of works they had turned to, abandoning his and showing that they had never savingly believed it, FOR THEY KEPT LOOKING TO THEMSELVES FOR THAT ULTIMATE ASSURANCE! **A gospel that conditions any part of salvation on a man doing something does not reveal that liberty wherewith Christ makes His people free, but rather a yoke of bondage** (see Gal. 5:1). Paul also told the Galatians, *"...if righteousness come by the law, then Christ is dead in vain"* (Gal. 2:21). The gospel that conditions any part of salvation on a work of obedience performed by man is a gospel that declares righteousness comes by *that* obedience, or is dependant upon *that* obedience, and therefore says that Christ died needlessly, that He need not have laid down His life, for the righteousness that saves a man comes by his own obedience and needed not to be supplied by a Savior. **Contrary to all this, the Scriptures say that righteousness comes by grace through faith in Jesus Christ and so any individual adherence to the law, believing that it will contribute to one's salvation, is that which is IN VAIN!** If anyone could be saved or sustain their salvation by what they did, surely at the head of that list would be the apostle himself. Yet Paul shows in Philippians 3:4-10 how he counts all things (all that he was and did) as loss *"...for the excellency of the knowledge of Christ Jesus my Lord....and be found in Him, not having mine own righteousness, which is of the law, but that which is through the faith of Christ, the righteousness which is of God by faith"* (Phil. 3:8,9).

Can you see that Paul is not dealing with the Galatians' 'good intentions' or sincerity of belief, but with the cold hard fact that if they looked to anything other than Christ and His Gospel as that which saves, then **whether they believed it or not, whether they were aware of it or not,** they held to another gospel, which cannot save? **Only Paul's Gospel demands that a person wholly trust in Christ for their salvation. That they wholly trust in the work**

of Christ because of the grace of God. Only Paul's Gospel demands complete abandonment of what we can do and complete reliance upon what God has done to save His people AND keep them saved. What the Galatians were being taught was a gospel that claimed to exalt Christ and yet included circumcision as part of, therefore essential to, God's great plan of salvation. **To exalt Christ one must believe His Gospel which conditions all of salvation on Him and that justifying righteousness is through belief in what He has done, not in anything that we must do.** For a person to be circumcised in order to ensure or secure their salvation, they must first have been taught such a thing and then believed in this false doctrine that was part of a false gospel, which dared add this religious work to the glorious Grace Gospel of God. Those who taught, and who even today continue to teach, such things—**adding anything to the Gospel message, or modifying it in any way**—in particular those who say that Christ's obedience must be supplemented by the personal obedience of each individual He died for, may not overtly deny any particular doctrine of the Gospel, or even be aware that they are, but by adding to it, by conditioning any part of salvation on what a man must do, they affect the whole and Christ shall profit them absolutely nothing. **Reliance upon one's own works instead of, or in addition to, what Christ has done is a rejection, it is a disapproval of the Gospel that declares**

"...His righteousness for the remission of sins..." (Rom. 3:25) and *"...that a man is justified by faith without the deeds of the law"* (Rom. 3:28). Just about every gospel out there that conditions salvation to some degree on what a man does is called a gospel of grace and is never termed a gospel of works. The 'grace' such promoters of false gospels are talking about is really a thin veneer—the superficial and pleasant appearance—behind which lies the backing material of *works*. **Their interpretation of grace is: God enabling a man to do in order to fulfil the conditions upon which they claim their salvation is based.** God's grace is not that which enables a man to obey certain conditions of salvation but it is God doing everything to fulfill every demand of His law and justice. *"...so by the obedience of ONE shall many be made righteous"* (Rom. 5:19). It stands as an eternal mystery why so many, who claim to believe in a gospel that gives God all the glory, refuse to believe that there is nothing they must do, no obedience they are to offer to God, in order to put a seal to their 'salvation'.

Christ is the Savior. And, if you believe that what He has done to save and keep saved all those for whom He died must be supplemented by something you do, some law you must obey, then you will always be looking to yourself and what you do to have that 'assurance' of salvation. REAL ASSURANCE IS FOUND ONLY IN CHRIST, AND ALL HIS PEOPLE ARE CONTENT WITH

HIM FOR THEY KNOW THEY ARE *"COMPLETE IN HIM"* (Col. 2:10).

The Scripture says that ***"...by the deeds of the law there shall no flesh be justified in His sight..."*** (Rom. 3:20). This justification, which no obedience to the law of God on man's part can ever attain to, is that which makes a man just before God AND KEEPS HIM THAT WAY FOR EVER!!! The righteousness which is of God, the only righteousness which saves, is ***"without the law"*** (Rom. 3:21). In other words, the righteousness by which a man is saved or justified cannot come, it is not attainable, by man's *deeds of the law* even if he says God helped him perform those deeds, but only ***"by faith of Jesus Christ"*** (in HIS deeds of the law) ***...For all have sinned, and come short of the glory of God"*** (Rom. 3:22,23). This is what salvation is all about isn't it? WHAT THE SAVIOR HAS DONE FOR THE SINNER!! Romans 4:6 describes ***"...the blessedness of the man, unto whom God imputeth righteousness WITHOUT WORKS."*** GOD DOES NOT NEED YOUR OBEDIENCE TO SAVE YOU!! **God justifies, He places a man in right standing with Him, not according to anything the man has done but according to everything God alone has done** (2 Tim. 1:9).

The fact that all have sinned precludes every last man from being able, by his own obedience, to gain or maintain a state of justification before God, for in everything a man does he always falls short of the glory of God and therefore of His approval. Men may appear righteous in the sight of other men, but none are righteous in God's sight by what they do, only by what Christ has done. The reason why **"...there shall no flesh be justified in His sight"** is the fact that **"...by the law is the knowledge of sin"** (Rom. 3:20). *"Law is a rule of action. The effect of applying a rule to our conduct is to show us what sin is (not how righteous we are). The meaning of the apostle clearly is, that the application of a law to try our conduct, instead of being a ground of justification, will be merely to show us our own sinfulness and departures from duty....so far from being justified by it, they would be more and more condemned."* The saved are **"...justified freely by His grace** (not by their works) **through the redemption that is in Christ Jesus"** (Rom. 3:24). Christ's righteousness does not only *get* a man saved, but what so many who profess to know Him have overlooked is the fact that His righteousness is also what *keeps* a man saved. **A man's salvation is ALL due to Christ, "Whom God hath set forth to be a propitiation through faith in His blood, to declare HIS righteousness for the remission of sins....that He might be Just, and the Justifier of him which believeth in Jesus"** (Rom. 3:25,26).

So many who claim to believe in the Gospel of Grace think that to be saved, to be justified, is a one-off thing and for the saved, justified state to be perpetuated or held on to, one must maintain a certain level of personal obedience. **While obedience is important in the**

believer's life, it is not a condition upon which salvation is based. Paul, bewildered, asked the Galatians, ***"Are ye so foolish? Having begun in the Spirit, are ye now made perfect by the flesh?*** (Gal. 3:3). Such people fail to realise that to be saved is to be *kept*, it is to be *preserved* and *protected from loss.* **Every bit of salvation, every bit of justification, is due to and because of Jesus Christ: Who He is and what He has done. Every bit of salvation is because of His obedience and not a bit of it is conditioned on your feeble attempts at obedience.** This Savior came to the earth to save His people from their sins because of the grace and purpose of God. **How ridiculous would it be for Christ to have come to the earth to get His people saved from their sins knowing they would all fritter away their salvation because of their inability and incompetence to remain saved by anything they did or could do! An inability Christ knew would never and could never sustain the justified state He had placed them in!**

"Christ did it all," you say? *"Christ is my all in all,"* you say? Then why do you think that any part of salvation is conditioned on you? Or why do you think that a person who believes such an abomination is saved as well as the one who rightly rejects it? And you who claim to now believe in the doctrines of grace, why do you insist that you were saved whilst believing such junk? **IF CHRIST DID IT ALL, THEN WHAT IS THERE LEFT FOR YOU TO DO?? If you claim Christ is**

your all in all then why are you believing in a gospel that conditions your salvation, even to the smallest degree, not exclusively and solely on what Christ has done, but also on what you do? HOW CAN ANYONE BE SAVED BELIEVING IN A GOSPEL THAT IS NOT TOTALLY, COMPLETELY, AND ABSOLUTELY, CONDITIONED ON GRACE? If you want Christ to be your Savior, if you dare to mention His name and think to call out to Him, *"HE IS TO BE A WHOLE SAVIOR. No one is to share with Him in the honor of saving men; and no rite, no custom, no observance of law, is to divide the honor with His death."* By changing even the smallest detail of the Gospel of grace, one does away with what **God has said** is required for salvation, replacing it with one's own version of what God has said. It is like adding the smallest mark to a beautifully painted white wall. No matter how small the mark, it has spoilt the purity of the whiteness, and the wall can no longer be considered *purely* white. One's eyes will virtually always be drawn to the blemish. **All that is required to blemish, nay totally do away with, the Gospel of grace is one single work of man's.** How can all of salvation be all of grace—all of God—if any part of it conditioned on what a man must do?

You see, the Message, or Gospel, of God is so perfect, so pure, so absolutely excellent, that once you change any part of it or fail to believe any part of it, you are left with another gospel and not that Holy Gospel of God. If you believe one doctrine of the

Gospel of God you must believe them all in order to truly believe His Gospel, for to not believe it all is to believe in things that contradict it. TO NOT BELIEVE IT ALL IS TO NOT BELIEVE IN GRACE! If you do not believe in God's Gospel of grace, which conditions **NO** part of salvation on man but **ALL** of it upon the Person and Work of the One Who was sent to save, the Lord Jesus Christ, you cannot be saved. If it is not **ALL Him it is not ALL grace** and can only be a gospel of works. You cannot spoil grace by adding grace to it for it is already grace and the Gospel of grace is perfect and complete. That which spoils, in fact cancels out, grace is called *works* even if it is claimed that God's grace is necessary to perform it. **A gospel of works is a gospel that contains a mixture of some of God's doctrines and some of man's doctrines.** If you go beyond the Gospel or fall short of it, if you abide in that which falls either side of what God has said, then you cannot have the Gospel of grace for your faith is found to not be within its boundaries. This is why, when there is error concerning the preaching of the Gospel, such erroneous teaching is termed *another gospel* and is not for a moment to be considered, as we see from Paul's writings, **God's** Gospel, and therefore as able to save. This is also what lies behind the reasoning in such verses as Proverbs 30:6: *"Add thou not unto His words, lest He reprove thee, and thou be found a liar"* (cf. Rev. 22:18). You cannot add grace to grace; you cannot make God's Gospel of grace any more gracious than what it already is. **The only way one can add to God's Gospel of grace is by conditioning any part of it upon a work of man's.** Anything added to what God has already said is **His** Gospel changes the message into a different gospel, just like adding even the smallest fraction to a correct answer to a mathematical equation changes that answer from being the right one to one of a multitude of wrong ones. For example, 2 + 2 = 4, but if you change that answer ever so slightly by saying that 2 + 2 equals 4¼, you no longer have the truth but are left with a lie. Even though your answer may contain the truth, what you add to it changes the whole into a lie, an untruth. **The most successful lies are not completely made up of untruths but contain mostly truth.**

THE INDISPENSABLE LINK BETWEEN MAN AND SALVATION IS GOD'S ONLY GOSPEL!! No other gospel can bring or hold the two together. God has only one answer to man's sin dilemma and it is revealed only in His Gospel of grace. A gospel preached and believed in that is not God's Gospel is a denial of God's Gospel, it is a rebellion against God's Gospel whether it is intended to be or not, and those who harbour such doctrines do in fact replace the true Gospel with what Paul called *another* gospel, *another* message, *another* plan of salvation, that is NOT God's plan, NOT God's Message, NOT God's Gospel. **All man has, in his natural state, is his version, GOD HAS THE TRUTH! All false gospels are merely pale imitations of the**

true one. **A FALSE GOSPEL IS A LOST MAN'S TRUTH.** All false gospels are *anti*-Gospel, for they are preached in its stead and are therefore against it. **All false gospels are perversions of the true Gospel and all who preach and believe a perverted gospel have a perverted view of God, and therefore a wrong view about how He saves. They are not true Christians but are themselves perverted versions who trust in a different plan of salvation than the one God has revealed in His Gospel. Their hope is in something other than what God has said and is utter vanity.** False gospels are man's attempts at outlining a plan of salvation and they are all miserable failures, for they have never saved anybody. Even one erroneous teaching, one false doctrine, added to the truth affects all of the right doctrines, just like a little leaven will always leaven the whole lump of dough. **Though there are many similarities among people, no two can be said to be exactly the same in thought or conduct. Every person is a unique individual. So, too, with gospels. Though false gospels may have some similarities, in some cases many similarities, to the true Gospel, not one of them can be said to be exactly the same and therefore we are left with only ONE that can save: GOD'S ONLY GOSPEL!!**

Just one false teaching will affect the true Gospel doctrines and leave you without God's Word on the matter. Dough is no longer purely dough if anything is added to it. Here is the essence of what Paul was trying to establish in the minds of those believers in Galatia. **Once you have changed the ingredients of the Gospel by either leaving some of them out or by adding to them or perverting them in any way, you no longer have THE GOSPEL but ANOTHER gospel, which is not that message, not that recipe, for salvation which God has specified in HIS Gospel.** To *corrupt* is to render a thing *"...meaningless or different in meaning from the original by scribal errors or alterations."* **False gospels are all meaningless nonsense for they differ from the original and only Gospel that saves.** Remember, only a little leaven is needed to leaven the entire lump! **Even one work which is said must be performed by man to either get saved or remain 'saved' frustrates the grace of God.** The apostle Paul said that he did not frustrate, or nullify, the grace of God by teaching that righteousness could come, or be sustained, by personal obedience, for this would then mean that Christ, the only one whose obedience *makes righteous* and *keeps righteous,* had died in vain (see Gal. 2:21). **Just one part of salvation conditioned on what a man must do rules out any claim for the gospel which teaches such a thing to be the Gospel of grace.** *"Erroneous doctrines are like leaven in the following respects: (1) They are, at first, slight and unimportant in appearance. (2) They are insinuated into the soul unawares and silently, and are difficult of detection. (3) They are gradual (4) They act most certainly. (5) They will pervade all* *the soul, and bring in all the faculties under their control."* A gospel which says man must perform a work, **even if it is vehemently insisted upon that the only way a man can perform the work is by the grace of God,** is a gospel of works not grace. To all who believe in such gospels there is only one thing left to say: ***"Christ shall profit you NOTHING!"***

THE CHURCH OF GOD

The very Foundation of God's Church, the people God has called out of the world to believe His Gospel and no other, is the doctrines of the apostles and prophets of God. All those who are now, and those who are to become, "...fellow citizens (true Christians) with the saints, and of the household of God;...are built upon the foundation *of the apostles and prophets, Jesus Christ Himself being the Chief Corner Stone"* (Eph. 2:20). The Foundation of the Christian Church is not the persons of the apostles and prophets but the Christ of their teachings: the Person and Work of the Lord Jesus Christ. **The Foundation of the Church of God is Jesus Christ as He is defined by, and revealed through, the Doctrines of the Gospel of the Grace of God in the salvation of His people through His Son the Lord Jesus Christ, the crucified and Risen Lord of Glory. The most important and integral part of the Foundation of God's Church is the Lord Jesus for without Him the edifice could not possibly stand, in fact, it could never even have been built.** *"Were it not for Him the edifice could not be sustained for a moment. Neither prophets nor apostles alone could sustain it."* The Church of God is founded upon the inspired teachings of the apostles and prophets concerning Jesus Christ and the salvation of God's chosen people. **The Christian Faith is NOT founded upon the teachings of mere men who know not God, nor is it founded upon the jesus of a man's imagination, but upon the true Jesus as he is revealed in the inspired teachings of God's chosen apostles and prophets.** Therefore to be **in** the Christian Faith, to be **of** the Church of Almighty God, is to believe in the doctrines upon which God's Church is founded.

"...the doctrines of Divine revelation, whether communicated by prophets or apostles, were laid at the foundation of the Christian Church. The Church of God was not founded on philosophy, or tradition, or on human laws, or on a venerable antiquity, but on the great truths which God had revealed....The Lord Jesus is called the **'Chief Cornerstone'**, *because the whole edifice rests on Him, or He occupies a place relatively as important as the corner-stone of an edifice."* "This phrase (cornerstone) is used by the Jews to denote excellency in a person; so a wise scholar is called (hnyp Nba) , 'a cornerstone'; see (Psalms 118:22) (Isaiah 28:16) (Zechariah 10:4) . It may be rendered, 'the chief cornering-stone'; it being such an one that is a foundation stone, as well as a cornerstone (see 1 Cor. 3:11); and reached unto, and lay at the bottom of, and supported the four corners of the building; for the

foundation and corner stone in this spiritual building, is one and the same stone, Christ: it is said of the temple of Latona, at Buto, in Egypt, that it was made, (ex enov) (liyou) , "of one stone", as Herodotus an eyewitness of it, attests."

To rightly teach the Gospel of Christ the Savior one must of necessity include all the doctrines of God's grace in the salvation of His people. To teach Christ aright, one must teach all the doctrines of grace that have to do with the salvation of God's chosen people for these doctrines show what was necessary for the salvation of God's chosen and by the same token reveal precisely what the Savior needed to do, and did do, to save God's chosen from their sins thus distinguishing Him as God's Son and the only one who came to save God's chosen from their sins. All the doctrines of the Gospel of God's Grace draw attention to and enhance the doctrines which specifically deal with the Person and Work of the Lord Jesus Christ, His Righteousness, which make up the Foundation of Truth upon which His Church stands.

The apostle Paul said he preached Christ and Him crucified (see 1 Cor. 2:2 & 2 Cor. 4:5), but to correctly do this Paul also preached the spiritually dead state of man, his complete inability to not only seek God, but to know Him (see Rom. 3); the grace of God; God's Sovereign election, made before the foundation of the world (see Rom. 9), of those God would entrust to His

Son (Jn. 17:2), etc. Paul also had to distinguish God's grace from man's works in that none would be saved who depended in any way upon what they did or did not do during the course of their lives. **That Christ would not profit such who looked to their own works as that which would in any way gain or maintain their salvation** (Gal. 5:2). Paul made it clear that God's people were chosen according to the election of grace and not according to their works (see Gal. 2:16; Rom. 11:7). **Therefore, the doctrines of grace, which negate any need for man to perform a work in order to be or remain saved, and which cannot be fully preached without the doctrine of election, which speaks of God's Sovereignty etc., are an essential Gospel matter which do not take away from the Person and Work of Christ, but enhance all that He is and all that He has done for all of God's people.**

THE CHURCH OF GOD IS FOUNDED ON THE LORD JESUS CHRIST WHO IS IDENTIFIED AND DISTINGUISHED FROM ALL OTHERS BY DOCTRINES (teachings) AND THESE DOCTRINES ARE COLLECTIVELY CALLED **THE GOSPEL OF GOD**. If one only has the doctrines which teach Who the Messiah is and what He has done, one does not have the whole Gospel. If one only preaches *'Jesus is the Savior Who died on the cross'* one is not rightly preaching Jesus Christ. **To rightly preach Jesus involves ALL the**

doctrines of the grace of God in the salvation of His people for these doctrines are all seamlessly woven together to spell out CHRIST. Key to Who Christ is and what He has done are the people for whom He has done it. Once you bring in the people for whom Christ died you are compelled by Gospel principle to speak of the spiritually dead state of man and his desperate need for a Savior, God's Sovereign Grace and the gift of Faith as well as God's Election of those people whom He would entrust to His Son and grant eternal life to, etc. **You cannot speak of what Christ the Savior has done without including whom He has done it for.** If you believe Christ's death was for every individual ever born then you are a subscriber to the satanic lie that all Christ has done on the cross is merely make salvation possible and not actual. To the lie that salvation is not reliant upon what Christ has done but ultimately upon a person's 'free will' choice to 'accept it'. If, however, Christ has died for an exclusive group of people (see Jn. 10:15), i.e., the ones God chose before the foundation of the world and entrusted to His Son (Jn. 17:2; Eph. 1:4), then what Christ has done on the cross is not merely make salvation possible but actual for all those for whom He died (see Hebrews 9:12,15).

    You cannot speak of Christ's death without teaching for whom He died for this is central to preaching and believing in the true

Messiah and the true Gospel which speaks of Him. Any who believe Christ has died for everyone does not believe in the effectual, substitutionary death of God's Son for God's people. If one only has all the other doctrines of the apostles but does not have the true doctrine concerning the Person and Work of Christ, one does not have the Gospel of God. **In fact, one cannot rightly believe in the other grace doctrines of the Gospel of God, if one does not rightly believe in His only Son.** One cannot rightly preach Christ without teaching the doctrines which define Him: Who He is, what He has done and for whom He has done it. **From this we learn that the doctrines of the Gospel MUST NOT be separated, for if they are, if even one of these doctrines is excluded from the preaching of the Gospel of God, the doctrines which are essential to a saving knowledge of God, then one no longer has the Gospel of God.** To take away even one doctrine from the Gospel is to take away from grace, what God has done to save His people from their sins. **The vacuum a doctrine of grace would leave could only ever futilely attempt to be filled by spiritually dead men through a work of their own.** For in the absence of grace, a Work of God's, there can only be a work of man's (see Rom. 11:6). One does not have the whole Truth of salvation by Grace through Jesus Christ, if anything which God has done to save His people is missing, neglected or omitted from His Gospel of grace. **One no longer has the true Foundation Stone.** The exclusion of vital doctrines, which are essential to the acknowledging of the Truth of God in the salvation of His people, such as election and God's Sovereignty, and whatever one preaches or believes in their stead, turns the Gospel into another gospel which cannot save. **A person either believes the truth, is ignorant of the truth and/or believes something other than the truth.** So if every Gospel doctrine which tells of the grace of God in the salvation of His chosen is not taught, then one gives place to ignorance. Moreover, if error is taught in place of the Truth of God then one gives way to the teaching and embracing of lies and the imperfect, erroneous, teachings of men, to false gospels which cannot save for they bear record of false gods and not the true and only God of grace.

In light of all this, can you imagine even one error being part of that which Scripture calls the Foundation of God's Church? **Can you imagine the words and teachings which are according to the traditions of mere men, resident in every false gospel and not the infallible teachings of the Word of God by His apostles and prophets, being the Foundation or forming any part of the Foundation of the Christian Church?** Or can you envision the Lord Jesus Christ being the Chief Cornerstone of the foundation of a false gospel? Of course not. **Then how, it may well be asked, can anyone rightly believe that a person is saved, or can be saved, whose house is built on a foundation that is not the Foundation of the doctrines of the apostles of which the apostles' Christ is the Chief Cornerstone?** How can anyone ever have been saved whilst residing in a house whose Foundation Stone is **not** Jesus Christ the Son of God?

God has not built His Church on any other foundation than that of the apostles and prophets, so how could God save anyone whose faith is grounded in doctrines that are simply not of God? The Lord God in calling His people out of the world into His Kingdom does not subsequently place any of His people in a house that is laid on any other foundation than that of His apostles and prophets, of which Christ His Son is the Chief Cornerstone! NO CHRISTIAN ABIDES IN A HOUSE BUILT ON A FOUNDATION OF SAND!! And no other house is built upon the foundation of the Gospel of Christ than the house which God has built. One cannot even be a Christian if the foundation of one's Faith is not the Word of God. **If one believes in lies, even in only one lie, concerning the doctrines of the Gospel of the grace of God how can it be rightly said that such a person is part of the Church of God which is built exclusively upon His**

Truth? If God did place at least some of His chosen ones in a house, or houses, built on sand, salvation would amount to nothing more than being moved from one house built on a flawed foundation into another house built on sand. It would be like being moved from one corner of darkness to another corner of darkness rather than being brought out of darkness altogether into God's marvellous Light (see 1 Pet. 2:9 & 2 Cor. 4:3-6). **All God's people reside in the house which God built upon the Foundation of His teachings about His Son.** Those who believe in false doctrines reside in another and are not saved. How can doctrines which teach a false christ be the doctrines which teach the true and only Christ? **How can the foundation of one house also be the foundation of another? How can those who live in one building rightly be said to be resident in another?**

Any doctrine, which deals with what God has done in the salvation of His people, which the apostles did not teach, or any doctrine that is in error concerning what they taught, cannot be considered part of the Church's Foundation or have any part in the Church's life. **False doctrines certainly play a major part in the life of the counterfeit church, in the lives of false brethren, but has no role in Christ's Church.** The Church of God is the pillar and ground of the Truth. It was built on the Truth of God, not on truth and lies BUT ONLY TRUTH. For a Christian - one who is called out of the world by God - to believe in only some of the true doctrines of the Gospel as well as false doctrines, would be tantamount to God having built His Church upon a foundation of rock *and* sand. A house built on sand will not stand. No part of the Foundation of the Christian Church, the teachings of the apostles and prophets, nor its Chief Cornerstone, includes within it any lie. **Therefore, the Church of God is called the pillar and ground of God's Truth for it is founded and built upon a pure Foundation of Truth. IT was born of Truth and created from Truth. So then, if the Church of God is, collectively, founded upon the Truth of God, then it must be that all the individuals that make up God's Church are also founded upon God's Truth for they are all *"...born again...of the Word of God...And this is the Word which by the Gospel is preached unto you"*** (see 1 Pet. 1:23-25).

    Literally the Church of God is built upon the Truth of God. Upon God's Word and NO other's. The life of every born-again Christian is built upon the Truth of God and NO other's. A foundation of rock does not fluctuate between being rock and sand, nor is it a mixture of the two. Likewise, the Christian Church does not fluctuate between truth and error, between what the apostles, prophets and the Lord Jesus Christ taught as God's Word, and the lies of men. **The doctrines of the True Gospel of God's Grace**

in Christ are the rock solid foundation of the Church of God. We see then that anyone whose faith stands, wholly or in part, upon a foundation of false doctrines, or on an incomplete gospel or a gospel made up of truth and lies, cannot be among those of the Church of God, because *those whom God has called out of the world* are built upon the Foundation of the whole Gospel Truth, all the doctrines which teach the grace of God in the salvation of His people.

There are only two foundations upon which one's life is built upon: (1) the Foundation of the apostles' truth about Who Christ is and what He has done, upon which the household of God is built, and, (2) the foundation of a false gospel, taught by those who are not part of God's household of called out ones but who reside in another building built upon another foundation, and which, therefore, speaks lies about Who Christ is and what He has done. Only those whose lives are built upon the only Foundation Stone which God has laid are part of God's Church. Is it then a fantastic thing to say that no one is saved who does not abide in the doctrines of the apostles, the only doctrines which testify of the true Christ? **The WHOLE doctrine of Christ must be believed in order to rightly claim residence in the household of God.** The apostle John shows that to not abide in the true teachings of the truth of Christ is to be without

Him and the Father: **"Whosoever transgresseth, and abideth not in the doctrine of Christ, hath not God. He that abideth in the doctrine of Christ, HE hath both the Father and the Son"** (2 Jn. 9). In writing to believers the apostle John also noted *"I have not written unto you because ye know not the truth, but because ye know it, and that no lie is of the truth"* (1 Jn. 2:21). Because of this John went on to say of himself and others who belonged to the Church of God *"WE are of God: he that knoweth God heareth us; he that is not of God heareth not us. Hereby know we the Spirit of Truth, and the spirit of error"* (1 John 4:6). No lie *"...either springs from it (the truth), or is according to it, but just the reverse. The apostle has respect to the errors and heresies of the above apostates, which were flagrant contradictions to the Gospel, and as distant from it as a lie is to truth; and of such lies, and of those liars, he speaks in the next verses. The Arabic version reads, 'and that every liar is not of the truth'"*. Christ says that any house built on a foundation of sand will fall (see Matt. 7). **Such is the foundation of error and such is the fate of all those who abide in the house upon which it is built.**

The Church of God, the Body of Christ, consisting exclusively of God's Gospel believers, should not 'be' the pillar of truth, as many wrongly preach, for **IT IS THE PILLAR OF TRUTH!!** All

Christians are part of *"...the house of God, which IS the Church of the living God, THE pillar and THE ground of THE Truth"* (1 Tim. 3:15), GOD'S TRUTH. The Church of God is not striving towards, nor is it aiming to become, the pillar and the ground of the Truth of God, for God's Word proclaims the Church of God **IS the pillar and the ground of the Truth of God <u>ALREADY</u>!!** WITHOUT THE TRUTH OF GOD THERE IS NO CHURCH OF GOD! THE CHURCH OF GOD PROCLAIMS THE TRUTH OF GOD. IF IT DID NOT DECLARE THE TRUTH OF GOD IT WOULD NOT BE HIS CHURCH. There would be nothing to distinguish it from counterfeit churches. **And, individuals who preach not the Truth of God are not of God and therefore could not possibly be part of His Church.** THEREFORE, WHAT THE CHURCH OF CHRIST, THE BODY OF GOSPEL BELIEVERS, PREACHES, IS THE TRUE AND ONLY GOSPEL OF GOD AND WHAT IT BELIEVES IS THE TRUE AND ONLY GOSPEL OF GOD AND NO OTHER! No other person but a Gospel believer can be part of the Church of Christ so what other Gospel could they possibly proclaim than the only power of God which is unto salvation: the Gospel of Jesus Christ!!**Therefore, how could anyone who believes in a false gospel possibly be within the Church of God? There are no false gospel believers in the Church of God for THE ENTRANCE WAY IS TOO NARROW FOR THEM TO PASS THROUGH.**

The Church of God is not a hybrid. All minds within it are sound and of one accord with what the Gospel of God is, and what it is not. Every member of it shares a belief in the same Gospel for they have all been given the same Faith with which to believe it. The Body of Christ is not divided for Christ says "...*if a house be divided against itself, that house cannot stand*" (Mk. 3:25). **The Church of God is not filled with diverse and contrasting beliefs about Who God is and what He has done in the salvation of His chosen. This is not a Scriptural description of the Church of God which is built upon the Foundation of Christ, but of a counterfeit church built on sand for a church divided against itself will not stand. God's House, His Church, DOES stand for it is built on His Truth, not on lies, or even a mixture of truth and lies, but on GOD'S TRUTH ALONE! Christ's people are unified, God's Church is one, for it is made up of Christians, the people who have been blessed to believe God's ONE Gospel with the ONE Faith God has given to each and every one of them which ENSURES they believe ONLY HIS Gospel.** What the apostle Paul said of himself may, with equal certainty, be said of all God's people: We are all **"...*separated unto the Gospel of God*"** (Romans 1:1). **This eternal separation<u>unto</u> God's Gospel is,**

simultaneously, and with equal certainty, an eternal separation <u>from</u> every false gospel.

How could Christians be the *"...ambassadors for Christ..."* (2 Cor. 5:20), **the same Christ upon which the Church of God is built, if they did not <u>all</u> believe the same, true and only Gospel of Christ?** If the Church of God, the people of God, are already the pillar and ground of God's Truth, as the Scriptures teach, then how could Christians teach and believe in any doctrine which differs with the doctrines of God's Gospel? How can God's Church be filled with a mixture of sheep and goats, of believers and unbelievers, when it is only the sheep who hear and recognize the Voice of the True Christ: *"...the sheep follow Him: for they know His voice. And a stranger will they not follow, but will flee from him: for they know not the voice of strangers....My sheep hear My voice, and I know them, and they follow Me: And I give unto them eternal life; and they shall never perish....Everyone that is of the Truth heareth My voice....And He shall set the sheep on His right hand, but the goats on the left....Then shall He say also unto them on the left hand, Depart from Me, ye cursed, into everlasting fire..."*(Jn. 10:4,5,27,28;18:37; Matt. 25:33,41). Everyone who is **of** the Truth **believes** the Truth. It is only the sheep of Christ who follow His Voice right into the household of God which is built upon the Foundation of the Good Shepherd.

    The Church of God, made up of the people God has chosen by grace from before the foundation of the world, IS the pillar and ground of the Truth collectively **and** individually, because they have all been blessed with the Faith of God to believe God's Truth. How could a single Christian not know or believe in the true Gospel of God and yet be in the Church of God's called out ones which is founded on the very Word, the Truth, of God of which it is the pillar and ground? **How could that which is the very pillar and ground of the Truth have even one member of it which did not know, or was in error concerning, the Truth? Christians all believe the same Gospel, for they have all been given the same Faith with which to believe it.** They are *"...with one mind striving together for the faith of the Gospel"* (Phil. 1:27 cf. 2 Cor. 13:11; 1 Cor. 1:10; 2:16; Rom. 15:5,6). The apostle Peter wrote ***"...to them that have obtained like precious Faith with us through the Righteousness of God and our Savior Jesus Christ"*** (2 Pet. 1:1). Paul the apostle made clear that ***"There is one Body, and one Spirit, even as ye are called in one hope of your calling; One Lord, <u>One Faith</u>, One Baptism, One God and the Father of all, Who is above all, and through all, and in you all"*** (Eph. 4:4-6).

If Christians believed in different gospels with the same Faith given to them by God, how would they differ from those unregenerate souls who believe different gospels with the faith that is common to man? If Christians believed in different gospels then God must have many gospels of truth, which in turn must necessarily contain different and contradictory truths for Scripture teaches that God's one and only Gospel is the Gospel of Grace. Seeing that grace is that by which God saves what further need would there be for several Gospels? **Christians make up that unique Body of people who know, believe and teach the Truth of God.** If Christians believed in opposing gospels then the Church of God would be the pillar and ground of the truth AND lies. **Since this is patently not the case it must be, as the Scriptures declare, that the Church of God is the pillar and ground of the Truth, therefore, there can only be one Gospel which rightly reflects God's Testimony of His Son which the Church of God, His chosen people, believe and proclaim:** *"He that believeth on the Son of God hath the Witness in himself: for he that believeth not God hath made Him a liar; because he believeth not the record that God gave of His Son"* (1 Jn. 5:10).

Contrary to popular belief, the Church of God is not some massive conglomerate made up of doctrinally differing denominations whose people attend gargantuan Gothic cathedrals some of which are even adorned with grotesque, demonic looking gargoyles and phallic-like steeples reaching up towards the sky. The Church of God is the assembly of *called out ones*, the ones who have been called **by the Gospel** out of error and into God's marvellous Truth ***"...to the obtaining of the glory of our Lord Jesus Christ"*** (2 Thess. 2:14). Those who are of the Household of God are: ***"...a chosen generation, a royal priesthood, an holy nation, a peculiar people; that ye should shew forth the praises of Him Who hath called you out of darkness into His marvellous Light: which in time past were not a people, but are now the people of God..."*** (1 Pet. 2:9,10).

"But we are bound to give thanks alway to God for you, brethren beloved of the Lord, because God hath from the beginning chosen you to salvation through sanctification of the Spirit and belief of the Truth: Whereunto He called you by our Gospel, to the obtaining of the glory of our Lord Jesus Christ" (2 Thess. 2:13,14).

REPENT AND BELIEVE THE GOSPEL OR YOU WILL DIE IN YOUR SINS

Please Contact:

morenodalbello@yahoo.com.au

Please Visit:

www.godsonlygospel.com

Made in the USA
Monee, IL
03 May 2026

49437973R00026